DATE DUE

The Discovery Books are prepared

under the educational supervision of

Mary C. Austin, Ed.D.

Reading Specialist

and Lecturer on Education

Harvard University

GARRARD PUBLISHING COMPANY
CHAMPAIGN, ILLINOIS

Henry Hudson

Captain of Ice-Bound Seas

by Carl Carmer

illustrated by John O'hara Cosgrave, II

To those intrepid explorers
Susie, Win and Duo Dickinson

Manufactured in the United States of America
Library of Congress Catalog Number: 60-11572

Contents

Henry Hudson: Captain of Icebound Seas

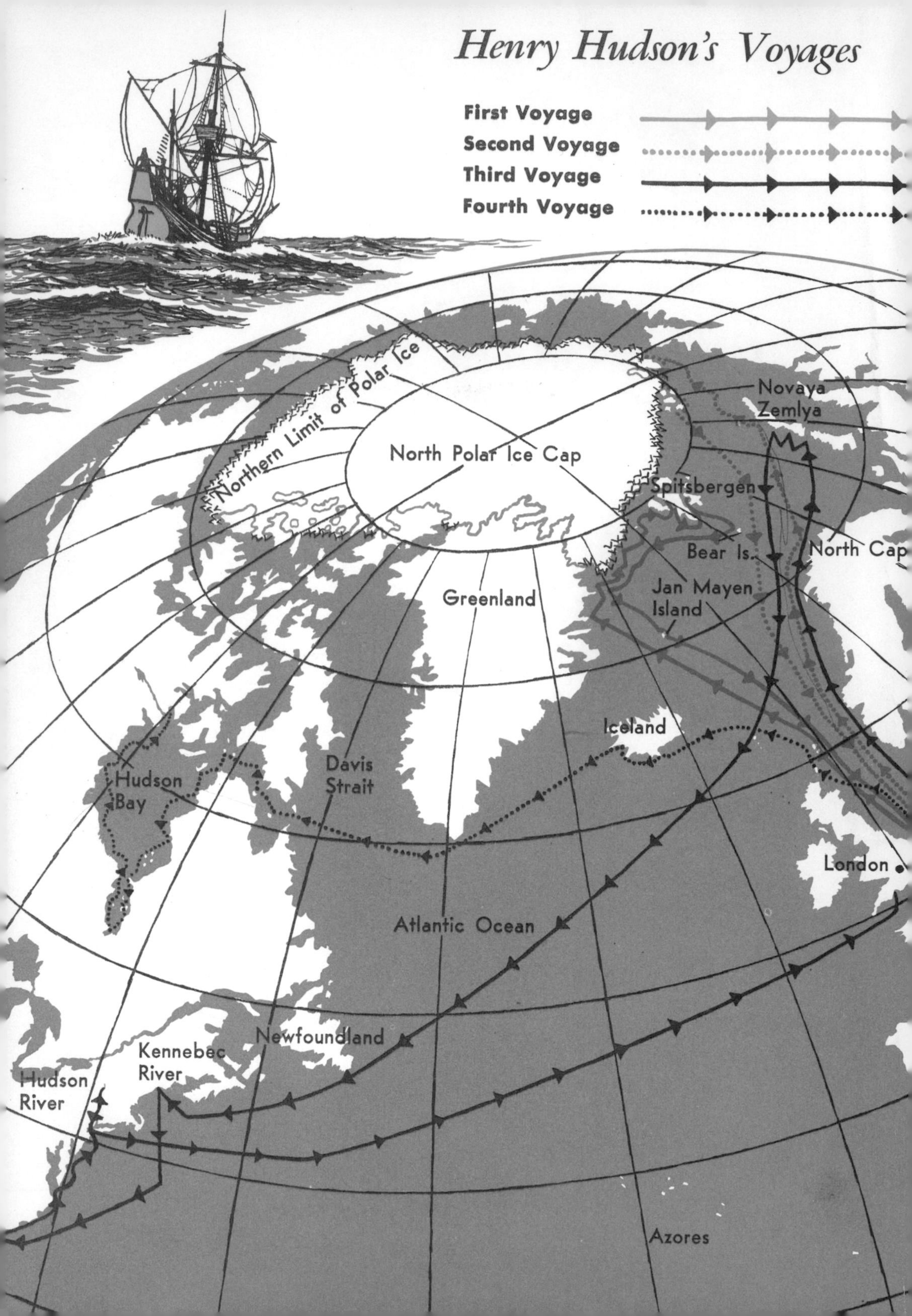
Henry Hudson's Voyages
First Voyage
Second Voyage
Third Voyage
Fourth Voyage
Northern Limit of Polar Ice
North Polar Ice Cap
Novaya Zemlya
Spitsbergen
Bear Is.
North Cap
Jan Mayen Island
Greenland
Iceland
Hudson Bay
Davis Strait
London
Atlantic Ocean
Newfoundland
Kennebec River
Hudson River
Azores

Chapter 1

Over the Top of the World

"Look Nick! That ship has come back! She left more than a year ago." Young John Hudson was talking to his friend, Nicholas Syms.

"Where do you suppose she has been?" said Nick.

The two boys stood beside the River Thames in England. This was the place in London they liked best. Something was always happening here.

"I see a monkey on the deck. The ship must have been to a faraway place," John said.

They saw a sailor catch the monkey and carry him away. Another sailor came on deck. A noisy, brightly colored bird sat on his shoulder. It screamed "Ahoy! Ahoy there!"

John and Nick laughed. "I wonder what else they brought back," Nick said.

"Probably they brought spices, tobacco and silk," said John. He already knew of the world beyond England. He knew that beyond the Atlantic Ocean lay a new land called America. And on the far side of America there was another ocean, the Pacific. He knew that across that ocean lay a far older land. It was a rich country called China.

"Nick," John said, "I want to go to China."

"Why, John, you would have to sail around the whole world! You would be gone for years!"

"My father says there is a shorter way. He says that instead of sailing around the world, you can sail over the top of it." John spread his arms out and bent his body from side to side. "I am a ship," he sang. "I'm sailing over the top of the world."

Nick did the same. Suddenly he stopped. In a whisper he said, "I can not move. I am icebound. There is nothing but ice in this north sea."

"No, Nick," John explained. "You are wrong. My father says the sun shines for five months at the North Pole.

So the sea there is warm. All we need to do is find a way through the ice into that sea."

"No one knows if that is true, John."

"My father will find a passage. Then we will know. He will find a short way to China."

"We'd better find the shortest way home," Nick said. "It is getting dark and I am cold."

"Good-by," laughed John. He ran all the way home.

"John, have you been at the river again?" asked his mother.

"Yes, Mother," he answered. "I love watching the ships. I wish Father would start his next voyage soon. I hope this time he will take me along."

John's little brother, Richard, said, "I want to go too."

John laughed. "You must grow up first."

The door opened and Captain Henry Hudson strode in. His oldest son, Oliver, was with him. John could tell from the way his father's blue eyes shone that something unusual had happened. Captain Hudson hugged his wife. "I have done it, Kate," he said excitedly. "I have the ship!"

John held his breath, waiting for his father's next words.

"The Muscovy Company wants me to find a short way to China."

"The Muscovy Company, Father? What is that?" asked John.

"A group of men, John, who trade with Russia. Now they want to trade with China too," Captain Hudson answered.

"Would that make them rich?" asked John.

"They hope so," said his father. "But finding new ways to new lands will help all men. It will help them to know and understand each other. That is better than riches."

"Take me with you, Father," begged John.

Captain Hudson looked at his son a long time. Finally he said, "Yes, you are old enough. You will have to work hard. But you are strong."

John was too happy to say a word.

Chapter 2

God's Blessing

Henry Hudson took John by the hand. They entered the church together. The bearded, blue-eyed Captain looked strong and sure. John Hudson stood straight beside him. He was proud of his father.

Ten sailors followed Henry Hudson and his son. They had come with their Captain to ask God's blessing on their dangerous voyage. It would be over waters no man had ever sailed before.

They knew they would need God's help. Only He could guide them.

The Captain and his son and the men knelt at the altar. A deep voice prayed for them. It said, "May God keep safe all men in peril on the sea."

The time when the sailors heard this prayer was more than three hundred and fifty years ago. The year was 1607. The day was April 19. After that the men worked hard. Finally their good ship *Hopewell* was ready to sail.

They pulled up the ship's anchor on May first. This was the day John had dreamed of. His eyes shone with excitement. The *Hopewell* drifted down the Thames River toward the ocean. John stood with the crew and waved to people along the banks.

The *Hopewell* soon left the fresh water of the river for the salty sea. Captain Hudson bravely turned the ship to the north. Cold, stormy winds blew against the sails. The ship's cat, Tom, meowed all the time. John could not make him come on deck.

John worked hard. He helped the cook. He carried food to the Captain and the officers. He kept the cabins clean. He learned to tie sailors' knots. He found out how to coil ropes on the deck. He was willing and eager to obey.

One morning the look-out man called from his seat on the main mast, "Land Ho!" John Hudson ran up on deck.

"What land is that?" he called to his father, who stood at the front of the ship.

"The Shetland Islands," said Henry Hudson. "Look closely. You will see the little ponies that live here."

"I want one," said John quickly.

His father laughed. "We will see many things you want before long. China is very rich. Some houses in China have roofs of gold."

"Can we take my mother a present made of gold?" asked John.

"We can."

"Then I will wait till later for my Shetland pony," said John happily.

Chapter 3

Whales at Play

The *Hopewell* sailed on northward. Now Captain Hudson had come to unknown seas. This was the chance he had wanted so much. He studied his books and his maps. He was excited and happy. The air grew colder. Big pieces of ice floated in the water.

One day John Hudson stood watch with seaman James Young. They were trying to see through a blanket of fog.

All at once Young called out, "Land Ho!" A narrow point of land stuck out into the icy water. It was right in front of the ship. John ran to warn the sailor at the helm. Together they changed the course of the *Hopewell.*

John held his breath. He was afraid the ship would run up on shore. But she slipped by into open water.

Captain Hudson called all the crew on deck. "Seaman James Young was the first to see this land," he said. "I will reward him for warning us. I am naming this cape Young's Cape." The sailors cheered.

The *Hopewell* now sailed north along the east coast of Greenland. Greenland is a long island northeast of Canada.

The ship ran into more ice. Her sails were frozen stiff. The crew was helpless on the icy deck. There was no sun. They could hardly tell day from night. Winds and high waves tossed the *Hopewell* about. She was driven away from Greenland. No one knew where they were. Days later the crew saw mountain tops ahead in a morning mist.

The ship had come to some little islands. A Dutch explorer had seen their high peaks years before. He had named them Spitsbergen, which means Pointed Mountains. The *Hopewell* sailed among these islands for many days. On July 14 she sailed into a small bay.

There the crew saw a great whale rise from the sea. It blew water high in the air. Then they saw another.

Before long the whole bay was alive with these big creatures playing together. The streams of water from their heads looked like fountains. The whales struck the waves with their tails, making showers fall upon the ship. They swam around the *Hopewell* as if they were asking her to play with them.

John Hudson laughed at them. Then he and the crew felt the ship lifted from the water. They ran to the rail and looked down. The largest whale had dived deep. Then, just for fun, he had come up under the *Hopewell's* bottom. The ship tipped to one side. It seemed about to turn over.

Captain Hudson shouted, "All men to the port side!" Quickly the crew climbed the slanting deck to the rail.

The whale swam away. The ship hit the water with a smack. No one laughed at the whales after that. They were too strong and too dangerous.

"I will call these waters Whales Bay," Captain Hudson said. "The big animals did not mean to hurt us. By God's mercy we had no harm."

Once more the Captain honored one of his men. "William Collins first saw the high land north of the bay," he said. "So I name it Cape Collins."

Captains before Hudson had taken credit for finding unknown lands. They did this even when their men had seen the lands first. Captain Hudson was more honest.

When they left the bay, the ship ran into very thick ice once again.

Still Captain Hudson ordered his crew to sail north. They moved along the coast called The Seven Icebergs.

The *Hopewell* was slowing down. Soon ice would stop her. It was getting thicker all the time. Captain Hudson knew he must go back to England before winter came. His blue eyes were sad. They saw only ice ahead. John came to his side.

"Father," he said, "next year we will find the way. We can always keep trying."

Chapter 4

No Luck

The *Hopewell* entered the River Thames in early autumn. John Hudson ran to his mother when he came ashore.

"I wanted to bring you a present made of gold," he said.

"I would rather have you back safe than all the gold there is," said his mother.

Nicholas Syms came to John's house to welcome him.

"So you did not sail across the top of the world," said Nick laughing.

"No," said John, "but we sailed farther north than any ship has ever been."

"Next time take me with you," said Nick.

"We need only one boy," John said, "and I am the boy."

Captain Hudson came in at that moment. He laughed at his son.

"Do not sound so important, John," he said. "Our voyage failed. We cannot be proud."

John hung his head.

Then his father spoke again. "But the Muscovy Company will send us again next spring," he said. "We will try again to find a way through the ice."

John jumped for joy. "We will do it! I know we will!" he said.

John counted the months eagerly. His father hired a new crew in March. He hired one man older than himself to be mate. The mate is the most important officer, next to the captain. This man was Robert Juet. He knew much about sailing, and he could write.

Captain Hudson was pleased with his choice. But John said to his mother, "I do not like the new mate. His eyes are small. He looks sly and mean."

"Hush, child," said his mother. "Your father knows best."

The *Hopewell* set out in April. As she sailed northward the weather grew foggy and cold.

One morning seaman Robert Raynor

shouted he could see a mermaid. Tom Hilles rushed to his side. Both men said this half-girl, half-fish looked at them earnestly. They said that from her waist up she looked like any human woman. She had long black hair and white skin. A wave turned her over and they could see her tail. It was like that of a porpoise but not so smooth. It was spotted like the tail of a mackerel fish.

Later on there were big blocks of ice floating in the water. The crew saw twenty walruses sleeping on an island. Captain Hudson sent his men ashore to kill them for meat.

They shot one walrus. The others jumped into the sea. The men also shot a large bird and gathered birds' eggs. That night they ate a big supper.

The next day the ice was gone. The *Hopewell* sailed into open water. For a time Captain Hudson thought he was near the North Pole. How happy he was! He thought he was sailing across the top of the world.

The Captain's happiness did not last long. Ice came again. It banged against the ship. The crew feared the *Hopewell* would get stuck in the ice. They would starve. Then the Captain showed them his maps.

"Look at these," he said. "They show we will soon be at the top of the world."

The crew said, "We do not believe you. The man who made the maps never saw the North Pole. We want to go home."

At last even Captain Hudson saw

they could sail no farther. He gave the order to return to England. John Hudson's eyes filled with tears. He ran to his father. "Don't be sad, Father," he said. "We can still try again."

But Captain Hudson said, "I have tried twice for the Muscovy Company. I have failed both times. They may not let me sail for them again."

The Captain was right about the Muscovy Company. When he returned to England the owners of the company scolded him. "You have wasted our money. You did not find China. We will not hire you to command another ship."

Captain Hudson said, "You are right. I failed you. But I know I can find the short way to China."

Chapter 5

First North, Then South

A company in another land had heard of the brave captain. It was the East India Company of Holland. The people of this little country are called Dutch.

The Dutch company asked Henry Hudson to come to Holland. There they made him captain of a ship named the *Half Moon*. They told him to go the way he had gone before. "Sail north," they said. "Cross through the ice into warm water. Sail across the top of the world. Then sail south to China."

Henry Hudson promised to try. But he did not tell his secret. Captain John Smith, who was his friend, had given him a map. Captain Smith had said, "If you fail to find a passage through the ice, use my map. Sail south to the coast of North America. I have settled a colony there called Virginia. When you reach Virginia, sail north. Follow the shore closely. You will see openings in the land. Sail into the widest. It may lead you from the Atlantic Ocean to the Pacific."

Hudson sailed the *Half Moon* from Holland on April 6, 1609. He followed the course he had taken twice before.

D'HALVE MAEN

Half of his crew were Dutch sailors. The Captain could not understand what they said. They often did not obey him because they knew no English.

John could not help laughing at the strange words. Robert Juet was a ship's officer again. He did not laugh at the Dutch sailors. He was angry when he could not understand them. John did not like Mr. Juet.

The *Half Moon* sailed north for two months. The fogs were the worst Hudson had ever seen. Dangerous blocks of ice floated near the ship. Strong winds blew. Many of the Dutch sailors had sailed only in warm southern waters. They hated the freezing weather which grew worse all the time. At last they refused to work.

The good Captain called his crew together. He told them he had changed his mind. He said no ship could get through the ice. No ship could reach the top of the world. He showed them the map Captain Smith had drawn. It might help them find a passage through the land. It might lead them to the Pacific Ocean, and then on to China.

The crew agreed to sail south. So Hudson changed the course of the *Half Moon.* Everyone was happy again, except Mr. Juet. John Hudson heard him talking secretly to the crew. "The Captain was wrong to think he could sail to the North Pole," Mr. Juet said. "This new idea of his is wrong, too. He can not find a way to China through the land."

John told his father what Mr. Juet said. Captain Hudson laughed.

"He may be right," he said. "We can find the truth only by trying many ways. One will turn out to be right."

The crew was not frightened by Mr. Juet. They wanted to find lots of gold in China. They hoped to get rich.

So they sailed on. A stormy wind broke their mast and the little ship sailed slowly. At last they saw land and tall pine trees growing beside a river. Now that river is called the Kennebec. It flows through the state of Maine.

The *Half Moon* sailed close to shore. The men were happy to see green trees after being so long at sea.

Even Tom, the cat, was excited. He ran back and forth across the deck. Mr. Juet stumbled over him. "Throw that cat overboard!" he said. "He gets in my way." But the cook hid Tom.

The men went ashore and cut down a tree. They made a new mast for their ship. Then they sailed south into the ocean.

Hudson kept studying John Smith's map. The little ship sailed on. Then one day he saw the white sand beaches of Virginia. He wanted to visit Captain Smith, but it was almost September. Winter would soon be coming and the water might freeze again. Hudson had little time. So he sailed north as Smith had told him to do.

The ship passed two wide openings in the land. Hudson decided these were places where rivers entered the sea. The map showed one more opening. He sailed toward it.

Indian dugout canoe

The cities and towns shown on this map did not exist when Henry Hudson sailed up the river that was later named after him. They are shown in order to give an idea of the size of the river.

The Hudson River

0 10 20 30

Scale of Miles

Halfmoon's small boat out ahead of ship sounding

Chapter 6

The Great River

Finally Captain Hudson sailed into a big harbor. He saw a wide waterway stretching far into the land. His heart beat fast. He would sail into it. Perhaps it was the short way to China. Then his dream would come true.

They anchored in the harbor. The next morning the Captain saw people in the woods along the shore. He sent men in a boat to bring them to him.

The people were Indians. They had been watching the *Half Moon.* They had never seen a boat larger than a canoe. Some Indians thought the ship was a big bird with white wings. Some thought it was a large fish. Others thought it was a floating house. They saw that the men in the house had white skin. The Indians looked at their own dark bodies. They said, "These white beings must be gods."

Henry Hudson put on a scarlet coat with gold buttons. He stood on the deck while the Indians climbed aboard. They sang songs to welcome the white men. They brought gifts of berries and corn. Captain Hudson spoke to them kindly.

Not all of the Indians were friendly.

Five seamen were rowing across the harbor just before dark. Indians in two canoes attacked them. An arrow struck John Colman in the throat. His friends tried to row him to the ship. They lost their way. John Colman died before morning came.

The next day Hudson's men captured two Indians. They locked them up. They hoped this would keep other Indians from attacking them.

Now the *Half Moon* was sailing up a broad stream. A high wall of brown rocks lined one side. On the other side the land sloped gently upward. It was covered with flowers and tall trees. Then the stream grew wider and wider. Captain Hudson thought it might end in a great ocean.

But farther along the waterway the stream became smaller. Mountains rose on either side. The Captain feared the stream was only a river after all. The *Half Moon* stopped. Captain Hudson ordered four of the crew to row north in the small boat.

"Find out if the water is deep enough for us to go farther," he said.

While the ship lay at anchor, the Indian prisoners wiggled through a porthole. They laughed as they swam to shore.

Soon some friendly Indians came on board. John was glad. These Indians helped his father forget his worries. The oldest Indian made a speech. John could not understand him. But he knew he must be a chief.

More Indians came aboard the ship bringing roasted deer meat. Captain Hudson ate the meat with the Indians.

When the visitors left, it was dark and beginning to rain. Captain Hudson walked sadly up and down the deck. At last the small boat returned. The men were wet from the heavy rain.

"Captain," said one of them, "the water north of here is shallow. The *Half Moon* can go no farther."

The Captain replied, "I have not found the short way to China."

"But Father," John said, "you have found a great river."

Captain Hudson did not know then that this river would become very important. He did not know it would be called the Hudson River.

The next morning Captain Hudson stayed in his cabin. He studied the maps spread out before him on his table. He drew lines on the maps.

"I must correct these maps before we leave," said the Captain.

Chapter 7

A Fight with the Indians

The *Half Moon* sailed back down the river.

One morning two canoes came alongside. In them were two old Indians and their wives. There were also two Indian girls. All came on board. The old men gave Captain Hudson some colored beads and tobacco. Captain Hudson gave them a knife which pleased them very much.

John wanted to talk to the Indian girls. But he knew they could not understand him. He liked the way they stood quietly while the men talked.

Almost every afternoon, when the ship had anchored, Indians came aboard. They brought fish and corn. In return Captain Hudson gave them knives and beads.

On the ninth day of their return trip, the river was very still. John watched the sun sparkle on the rocky shore. His father was in his cabin working on the maps. Captain Hudson was upset about his failure. John knew he did not want anyone to talk to him.

Suddenly John saw two canoes. They were not like any he had seen before. The Indians in them came on board.

They did not seem friendly. They rudely picked up everything they could to show to each other. One of them spoke to John. But John did not know what he said. The Indians laughed and John's feelings were hurt. The Dutch sailors got together. They were talking quickly. They did not like these Indians. Everyone was glad when the Indians left the ship. They paddled their canoes around the *Half Moon.* But they did not go away.

"Shall I call my father?" John asked Mr. Juet.

"No. He does not wish to stop his work. And so far the Indians have done no harm."

The crew stood around watching the canoes. Some of the men had their guns. John could tell they were afraid.

John walked to the back rail of the ship. He saw an empty canoe. Then he saw a pillow thrown into it. He leaned over the rail as far as he could. An Indian was hanging on to the rudder of the ship. John saw the Indian put his arm in a window. He pulled out two shirts and threw them into the canoe. Then he jumped in and started away.

"Wait," John called loudly. "Come back!" Just then Mr. Juet fired his gun at the Indian. The bullet killed him.

Men were rushing around on the deck. Some got into the little boat. They had guns and big knives. John jumped into the boat as it pulled away from the ship.

The Indians were afraid. Some of them paddled swiftly toward shore.

Some jumped from their canoes and started to swim toward the land.

The ship's crew only wanted to get back the pillow and the shirts. They grabbed them from the drifting canoe. Then John saw an Indian swimming toward the boat. The Indian put his hand on the edge and pulled. He was trying to turn the boat over. It rocked from side to side. Water came in. The cook drew his big knife and struck the Indian's hand. The Indian fell back into the river yelling. John had never heard such a horrible cry. By the time the boat got back to the *Half Moon,* the Indians had gone.

Captain Hudson was on the deck.

"Mr. Juet," he said sharply, "why did you kill that Indian?"

"He stole my shirts," said Mr. Juet.

"That is no excuse for murder," said Captain Hudson. "We will leave this place at once. I want no more trouble with Indians."

Chapter 8

Homeward Bound

Captain Hudson did not get his wish. The next day an Indian tried to come aboard. He was one who had been there the day before. Other Indians were in canoes on the river.

The sailors would not let the Indian come on deck. The other Indians were angry. They picked up their bows. They shot arrows at the crew. One arrow came close to John. It made a whizzing sound. The sailors fired at the Indians.

But they did not go away. More Indians appeared. John grabbed a gun and fired it. Bang, bang, bang!

Indians whooped and yelled. Guns banged. No one could hear the Captain's orders. Suddenly the Indians went away.

Again the Captain ordered the men to sail on down the river. John picked up three arrows from the deck.

"I will take one for each of my brothers. And I will give my mother one," he said.

In early October the ship came to the river's end. John was sorry. The river was a great river. Tall trees grew on its banks. Their leaves were red and yellow in the clear air. Sunlight made the water glisten. John had liked the river. He had even liked the Indians.

The *Half Moon* sailed into the harbor. Beyond lay the ocean and then home.

"Men will hear of these waters and this rich land," said Henry Hudson to his son. "They will come here to live. A big city will rise where the river meets the ocean."

He did not know it would be the greatest of all cities. He did not know it would be the City of New York. He did not dream that ships would crowd the harbor. He could not know it would be the world's busiest port. It would become New York Harbor.

Chapter 9

The Last Voyage

At last the *Half Moon* docked safely in England.

The King heard about the rich lands Hudson had found. He ordered the Captain not to leave England. He said the Dutch crew could take the *Half Moon* back to Holland. He said Captain Hudson must work only for his own country.

Three rich Englishmen made Hudson captain of a ship named *The Discovery*.

Now he would have another chance to find the short way to China. He left England on April 17, 1610. Again he took John and Mr. Juet with him. He let John's friend, Nicholas Syms, go too. John thought two boys would have more fun than one. Most of the crew were tough, mean men. Only a few were friendly to the Captain.

They sailed north. Hudson had heard of a new sea that another explorer had found. It was near the northern shores of the land we now call Canada.

In June they stopped off the coast of Iceland. John and Nicholas found hot springs on the shore. Everyone bathed in the hot waters. They caught fish and birds to eat.

In July, Captain Hudson sailed *The Discovery* between two high mountains into a great sea. He was sure this was the short way to China. He did not know it was only a large bay. Today it is called Hudson Bay.

For a month everyone was happy. The ice was not too thick. There were polar bears on an island. The crew chased them. John and Nick yelled as they ran after the big white bears.

Hudson sailed *The Discovery* first north, then south. He kept running into land. The shore was level and brown. Its dead grass rattled in the wind. The unhappy crew wished to go home. They began to quarrel. But the bold Captain would not give up his search.

The ice in the sea became very heavy. In November it stopped the ship. The men anchored near the shore. Soon the ship was frozen in by ice. They had only food enough to keep them alive. Everyone was hungry, and there was nothing to do. Many men were sick. Often they would not obey their Captain.

Mr. Juet again talked against Henry Hudson. "Everybody might die," he said. "It's the Captain's fault. Hudson should not be Captain."

Juet said, "I am older than Captain Hudson. I am wiser. I have spent more time at sea. I would never have brought you to this awful place."

At first the sailors would not listen to him.

Then Juet said, "The Captain stays in his cabin. We can't see what he does. Maybe he eats more than his share of food. Perhaps he has hidden some."

The men began to whisper among themselves. John Hudson heard them. He told his father, "I am afraid of Mr. Juet."

Captain Hudson had Mr. Juet brought before him. The Captain said, "You are on trial for being disloyal." A man told what Juet had said. Then the Captain told Juet, "You are no longer an officer of this ship. Someone else will take your place."

Mr. Juet was very angry. All winter he said more unfair things about the Captain. The men began to believe him.

They wondered if the Captain was stealing food. They were hungrier than ever.

Spring came at last. The ice began to melt. Soon they could go. But by now only a few men trusted Hudson. One day, Mr. Juet met with the crew secretly. "We will get rid of the Captain," he said. "Then we will sail home."

They made their plans.

At sunrise on June 22, Captain Hudson stepped from his cabin. Some men grabbed him and tied him with rope. The men had guns and knives. John ran to his father. He called Nick. Mr. Juet ordered, "Stand back, Nick."

The men brought the ship's small boat alongside. They put Captain Hudson in it with six of the sick men.

Then John got into the boat. He would not leave his father.

Phillip Staffe, the ship's carpenter, came on deck. He said to Mr. Juet, "You have done a wicked thing. Bring those men back."

"No," said Mr. Juet. "This ship is mine!"

"Then give me my tools," said Mr. Staffe. "I would rather die than sail with men like you." He got into the little boat with his tools.

"Mr. Staffe," said Captain Hudson, "you are loyal and brave."

Nick ran to the ship's rail. He was holding Tom, the cat, in his arms. "Good-by, John," he shouted. "Good luck!"

"Good-by, Nick," shouted John.

Then Mr. Juet cut the rope of the small boat. It was set adrift. In it were the Captain, his son John, Mr. Staffe, and the six sick men. They had no food and little clothing. They sat in the boat shivering. They saw *The Discovery* sail away. The ship was soon out of sight. They were alone in the icy sea.

Chapter 10

What Happened Afterwards

The men on *The Discovery* soon needed food. They went ashore to hunt. Eskimo Indians shot arrows at them. The men ran for the ship. But four of them were killed. Only a few men were left. They began sailing back to England. Their food gave out. Old Robert Juet died because he did not have enough to eat.

When *The Discovery* reached England all of her crew members were arrested.

The men said Hudson had stolen their food. They also said they had found the short way to China. Nick said this was not true. But people believed the sailors. They were not punished.

A ship was sent to look for Henry Hudson and his eight companions. But no trace was found of them.

No one knows what happened to Henry Hudson. But sixty years later, a French explorer found a ruined house near Hudson Bay. It looked as if it had been built by an English carpenter. People remembered that Mr. Staffe, *The Discovery's* carpenter, had stayed with Henry Hudson. Perhaps the Captain and John had lived there. Perhaps all those in the little boat lived on the Bay.

Perhaps they fished and hunted for years beside the waters of Hudson Bay. Perhaps they met friendly Indians.

We do not know. Whatever happened, we do know that we remember Henry Hudson. We know a great river was named for him. We know a great bay was named for him. We know ships enter the bay through Hudson Strait. Henry Hudson was one of the world's bravest explorers.

Other Books for Young People by
CARL CARMER

PETS AT THE WHITE HOUSE

AMERICA SINGS

HURRICANE LUCK

THE WINDFALL FIDDLE

THE SCREAMING GHOST
(and Other Stories Collected and Told by Carl Carmer)

A FLAG FOR THE FORT

WILDCAT FURS TO CHINA

TOO MANY CHERRIES

EAGLE IN THE WIND

HURRICANE'S CHILDREN

Edited by Carl Carmer

CAVALCADE OF AMERICA

CAVALCADE OF YOUNG AMERICANS